MW01505992

DIY Spirituality

DIY Spirituality

CHART YOUR OWN SACRED PATH

By Faith Freed

ART BY DORIANA DEL PILAR

THE
collective
BOOK STUDIO

Library of Congress Cataloging-in-Publication Data available.
ISBN: 978-1-68555-284-8
Ebook ISBN: 978-1-68555-796-6
Library of Congress Control Number: 2025902886

Manufactured in China.

Edited by Marisa Solis
Art by Doriana Del Pilar
Art Direction and design by Rachel Lopez Metzger

10 9 8 7 6 5 4 3 2 1

The Collective Book Studio®
Oakland, California
www.thecollectivebook.studio

For new adults.
Because figuring it all out is no small task.

TRACK LIST

Welcome to the Divine Party

Greetings, cosmic celebrator. Welcome to this little launching pad and rock 'n' roll rocket ride to an elevated experience of life!

If you get that there is more to existence than meets the eye, consider this a divine high-five. Have you got a deep knowing that you're held and adored by the same all-encompassing force expansive enough to also cradle the mountains and stars? Do you sometimes get the feeling we aren't making a big enough deal of this? What could be a bigger deal, actually?

You feel connected in some cosmic way to all that is. But what are you supposed to do with that? Maybe you're wondering exactly how to honor your absolute sense that spiritual forces are at play in your life. Maybe you have a solid spiritual life and you're ready to take it to the next level. Or perhaps you want to explore your own authentic path but aren't sure how to go about that. If you could benefit from a framework for do-it-yourself spirituality, this book found you right on time.

How do you connect with your spiritual source? How do you light your inner spark? Where do fiercely authentic seekers—from doubters to devotees—turn for a structure to build upon? What is the glue that binds your custom collection of wisdom, beliefs, and routines? Your method of incorporating spirituality into your life regularly can be called your spiritual practice, or *practice* for short. If you don't necessarily have the functional application all figured out, yet you sense that without some attention to a spirituality that resonates, you may miss out on your next-level life, this book will serve as a homebase to contemplate and consecrate, whatever that means.

What Rings True to You?

You might say spiritual freestylers have been ignored, with little support and few tools available to them. And yet, you're everywhere, doing your own spiritual thing independently, because that's how you like it. No rules. Just whatever rings true. It can feel a little confusing, though. What's out there doesn't necessarily fit, but that's no reason to give up on faith, right? Faith is an underutilized and valid antidote to fear, which shows itself in all kinds of forms: stress, anxiety, depression, and dream-crushing self-doubt. There's something so reassuring about connecting with your spirituality, whether you choose to do so solo or in the company of your tribe, online or in the flesh. The options are limitless, but it does help to have a plan.

That's where this book comes in. Think of *DIY Spirituality* as a framework for your divine practice. Nope, this book isn't gonna tell you what to believe or what to do, even if you play it backwards on vinyl. That's for you to figure out. Rather, *DIY Spirituality* offers you a way to organize and customize your practice so it fits *you*. It helps you deepen and widen your do-it-yourself practice. Best of all, it shares several simple, soul-engaging activities you can try out—or not, because it's your life, your mashup, your show.

Unleash Your Uniqueness

If DIY spirituality seems daunting, think of your spiritual path as something that's being revealed, rather than a direction you're forced to choose. Be open and curious as you explore what spirituality means to you and how to set up a practice so it becomes a habit. The ideas in this book are meant to help you unleash your unique spirituality, not to create a calculation for how to do life. You may find that simply anchoring your life in something meaningful, while staying aware of the wonders around and within you, keeps you in the zone—grateful, enthused, and in the moment—a lot more often.

As you explore the resources on offer in this book, lean into whatever works for you. Obviously, if it doesn't fit, fast forward. Now, let's prep to get this party started.

Your Spiritual Playlist

So what is *spirituality*? Think of it as an intentional quest to connect with the source of all that is and with your own true essence within. Hello? Kind of important. Spirituality differs from religion in that the connection is what's emphasized, not so much the way one goes about connecting.

Feeling lost while exploring spirituality is normal. It's not like solving a math equation. There's no exact right answer. Asking questions may be the cornerstone of the beginning, the middle, and the destination of your spiritual journey. Curiosity about the eternal, ethereal, and unknowable shows intelligence, as in, *Ya don't know what ya don't know.* And humility, as in, *Even geniuses admit we can't explain it all.*

Whether a spiritual path is inspired by a religious tradition, forged by your own ingenuity, a remix of what works based on trial and error, or all of the above, you're golden. Because, essentially, you're creating your own spiritual playlist. Do you have a favorite genre of music that makes you feel good? Transcendent, even? Can you even sit still when that house beat drops? Or maybe a country song or breakup ballad hits you hard on the heartstrings? And how can you not hit the floor when you hear your fave throwback tracks? What makes one person's spirit soar is different from what lights up another's. What's imperative is that you get to enjoy music.

Spirituality is like the music itself, rather than the particular genre or song. What matters isn't so much how you connect with your divine self and source at a given time, but that you connect. It can be easy to cultivate your own rich and rewarding relationship with your spiritual source, as you conceive of it, without undue complexity, inaccessible language, or hierarchical authority figures. Ultimately, it's not the religion that matters; it's the relationship. So go ahead, sample some divine tracks to follow. Just like music, you don't know what you like until you hear it. So you're free here to consider some expressions of spirituality that you may or may not care to incorporate. In this book, you'll be invited to make your own spiritual playlist based on what divine frequencies resonate at your core.

Mahatma Gandhi once said, "I consider myself a Hindu, Christian, Moslem, Jew, Buddhist, and Confucian." And why shouldn't key elements of different faiths harmoniously coexist? The areas of overlap transcend form and point to the truth connecting us all. You're free to take what works from each tradition and add your own twist; after all, your beliefs might as well be every bit as colorful, dynamic, idiosyncratic, and evolving as you are as an individual. Whether you embrace the tradition of your ancestors, adopt a different tradition, dabble with some eclectic combination, or create a spirituality of your own design, what matters is the relationship between Self and Source.

Calling Your Creator

Most likely, the essential energy of "being" doesn't care what it's called. What you call your creator is your call. There are many perfectly good names: Higher Power, Spirit in the Sky, The Universe, The Force (I see you, *Star Wars* fans), and the OG handles God and Goddess, ad infinitum. Within this book, we'll go with *Infinite Source*, or *IS* for short. Not by accident, "IS" is also the word used to describe the state of being. IS—it's as simple as it gets and it captures all that is, right now.

Infinite Source is the essence of everything that exists. This entity or energy isn't easily defined. Within or without a construct, the individual conception of a higher power is highly personal. So how this makes sense to you (or how it doesn't) has everything to do with your interpretation. Intentionally or not, you put your own spin on faith, as it should be.

If the name IS doesn't work for you, swap it for your own term for the Divine. Or ditch the name game altogether. When it comes to spiritual material, this bite-size book included, you're free to simply take what resonates and leave the rest. When something doesn't fit, hit skip. Don't overthink it. Have fun with it. Keep it light, party people.

The Multifaceted Face of DIY Spirituality

In order to bring your faith into practice, it's useful to have a philosophical framework from which to start. With some structure, you can integrate spirituality on a daily basis. To get the ball rolling, here's a simple yet celebratory system to support your DIY spirituality: *The Divine Disco Ball.*

   This dazzling centerpiece, which we'll explore in detail in Track 2, consists of four distinct quadrants that make up a whole. Each colored section represents an essential way that IS illuminates existence. We will explore each quadrant, one by one. This framework is meant to serve as an example of and inspiration for any DIY spiritual practice. As this sparkly orb catches the light, may it also capture your attention as a playful reminder of the extraordinary energetic influences at work all around you and within you!

Spin It Your Way

When it comes to faith, only you can say what's true for you. You're free to do whatever makes sense—and Jack, Jill, Sawyer, and Socorro can do the same, with mutual respect. Maybe the ideas that follow will reinforce your beliefs, or maybe they'll prompt an open-minded exploration of your faith. Maybe they'll complement the ingredients already in your spiritual soup. Whatever you get out of it, it's personal—just like your relationship with Infinite Source. If you've ever been in a relationship, you know it's complicated.

That said, this framework for do-it-yourself spirituality, emblazoned by the Divine Disco Ball, is served straight up. You're free to use it, modify it, or start from scratch with your own DIY framework. No matter your approach, make it your goal to empower yourself, ignite your inner flame, and begin to foster a direct connection with Infinite Source. And have a blast while you're at it! Rumor has it, IS loves to celebrate.

Connection to a higher power is an equal-opportunity endeavor. There is no gatekeeper to god/dess. So forget about getting permission from any alleged guru and go for it. Or don't. Do it your own way. Or don't. No preaching. No proselytizing. Just your very own personal truth with which no one can argue.

The Divine Disco Ball

Whether you're a sun worshipper or prone to dancing in the moonlight, you have to admit, there's nothing like light to turn us on. A fiery orb in the sky will do it. So will a sparkling sphere rotating high above a dimly lit dance floor pulsing with your favorite beat. A disco ball projects and reflects light out onto you and your fellow revelers. The spirit it stirs is joy. The invitation it commands is to commune in high energy. The sparkles it flashes radiate joie de vivre. Irresistible tunes, impressive moves, and reflective gleams combine in a dance of appreciation for life and all that IS. That's the power of the Divine Disco Ball. It can ignite your inner flame and prompt you to shine brighter.

The dynamic nature of existence is reflected in the form and function of the Divine Disco Ball: colorful, cyclical, kinetic, and electric. Dazzling and multifaceted, it also mirrors us complicated creatures. Disco balls are retro rotating globes, just like our cosmic dance floor, Planet Earth.

The Divine Disco Ball is also paradox in form, winking at the inevitable contradictions at play in life. Both a tribute and a toy, the Divine Disco Ball is to be taken seriously as well as regarded lightly. It's a sacred symbol, and at the same time, it's simply a vintage ornament inspiring fun and frolic. It's up to you what you make of it, if anything. Like life, the Divine Disco Ball holds the meaning you ascribe to it. It's reverent and/or irreverent, depending on how you see it. Like most people, it's simultaneously both. And you thought it was all about ABBA. Mamma mia!

Breaking It Down

Now, let's break it down. The Divine Disco Ball is composed of four parts. Each of these quadrants is an aspect of existence and all that IS.

The FAB FOUR

INFINITE SOURCE
(HIGHER POWER)

INFINITE SELF
(HIGHER SELF)

INCARNATE SOURCE
(NATURE)

INCARNATE SELF
(BODY-MIND)

The Cosmic Axes

The Divine Disco Ball is divided along a vertical axis: The left side of the ball is devoted to Source, and the right side is devoted to Self.

SOURCE = spiritual force that animates existence and informs what is

SELF = your whole being—physical body plus soul/spirit

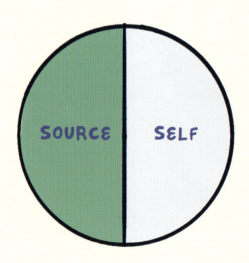

The Divine Disco Ball is also divided along a horizontal axis: The top represents the Infinite, and the bottom represents the Incarnate.

INFINITE = nonphysical, unseen, ethereal aspect of spirituality
INCARNATE = physical, seen, embodied form of spirituality

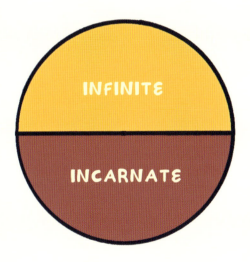

You probably already grasp the awesome meaning of the word *infinite*: boundless, immeasurable, utterly without limits. This book uses "Infinite" more along the lines of the definition of *ineffable*, which means beyond words, celestial, divine, ethereal, ideal, indescribable, transcendent, and too sacred for words. In this case, think of Infinite as aspects of existence you feel or even know, but can't see or prove. Imagine the rush you get when, say, the sweetest, most adorable puppy wags its tail and jumps in your lap. Your body is flooded with feel-good juice. With IS, that feeling is raised to the nth degree. It's surely meant to be. Beyond just feelings, these fundamental qualities of life are very real, yet elusive.

If you're more of a cat person or you're weirdly not into cute animals, consider the miracle of an uncanny collision: how a divinely orchestrated "chance" encounter led to a new home, a dream job, or an epic love affair. Infinite is what we mean when we say, "The stars aligned."

Some of us are more in touch with the infinite qualities of life than others. Very rational types might not buy the idea that anything exists beyond what can be proven. But great scientists—indeed, Albert Einstein himself—have acknowledged the mysterious and hidden aspects of the universe. Einstein wrote: "Try and penetrate with our limited means the secrets of nature, and you will find that behind all the discernible concatenations, there remains something subtle, intangible, and inexplicable. Veneration for this force beyond anything that we can comprehend is my religion. To that extent, I am, in point of fact, religious." The inexplicable secrets of nature to which Einstein refers could be considered Infinite.

Now that you get what Infinite means in the context of the Divine Disco Ball, it'll be easy to understand the term *Incarnate*. Basically, it's the opposite of Infinite. Incarnate is that which is embodied, physical, and manifest. Externalized and tangible, this is the form we experience with our five senses (the sixth sense is just a bonus). It's the skin you're in and the planet where you play. It's thoughts and thunder, bones and bedrock. Incarnate encompasses your amazing body and Earth in all its natural beauty.

The Cosmic Quadrants

Let's take a quick look now at the meaning of each quadrant of the Divine Disco Ball and its corresponding color spectrum. We'll give a token nod to convention and explore the orb clockwise. Once the basic ideas are clear, we can move fluidly among the quadrants, as we do in life.

We begin in the upper-left quadrant, with *Infinite Source*. This part represents the ineffable aspect of the divine, or Source unseen. It's the animating life force and ultimate essence of all that exists. It's the great mystery, the unfathomably gifted creative behind the curtain. The silver mirrorball catches the light and radiates energy. It also clearly reflects the divinity in you, your fellow celebrators, and the purity of all that is.

Moving to the upper-right quadrant, you'll find your personal ineffable aspect: the *Infinite Self*. This represents your higher self, the divine in you. Think of it as your timeless spirit/soul or god/dess within—that essence of innocence and wisdom you were born with. This part on the Divine Disco Ball represents the bright flame of your inner spark. Warm golden hues point to your essence, aka your lit-up radiant Infinite Self.

Moving down, the lower-right quadrant is your sensual *Incarnate Self*: you, embodied. This aspect includes your body, mind, ego, and personality. Basically, it's the sexy package you put forth and use to function. This part blends passionate, vibrant hues of purple and red,

representing physical vitality, with shades of their soothing, lighter counterparts, reflecting a tamed, transcendent mind. It may serve to remind you of your highest consciousness and the bold heart-centered body that keeps you dancing.

The lower-left quadrant, *Incarnate Source*, represents nature, the divine in physical form. Incarnate Source includes everything observed in the wondrous natural world: air, water, trees, creatures, sky—all of it. This is the divine force that visibly animates our planet and the physical evidence of Infinite Source. This aspect is represented by hues of green and blue on the Divine Disco Ball to represent our lush and lovely playground: planet Earth.

Spiritual Spin

If you're starting to get how each quadrant of the Divine Disco Ball corresponds to an aspect of spirituality, then you're probably also beginning to see how each part might be applied to your own spiritual gig. That's the whole point. This framework is designed to help you stay aware of four fundamental aspects of your spiritual life, thus enabling you to see infinite possibilities, spot opportunities for growth, and feel aligned, ignited, and divinely inspired. Touching upon each quadrant allows you to gain balance when needed, go deeper when desired, and express gratitude on the daily.

Elevate Upward

There are lots of ways to spin this ball, once you sample it. You might find it useful to consider how the top half is infinite, reminding you to go vertical when life is getting you down. Elevating upward and connecting with Source toward the starry sky can restore your spirit and sprinkle you with celestial guidance.

Ground Yourself

Then there are times when it's all too much. The swirls of big questions, chronic issues, and challenging personalities can throw you off your center. When that happens, you need to find your deep roots into the Earth. Venture south on the Divine Disco Ball and anchor back into your party planet. Go barefoot and sink your ten hard-working toes into the grass or floor beneath your feet to get grounded again.

Hang a Left

You might consider how the horizontal line of the Divine Disco Ball allows movement between Source and Self. Too much time on the Self side can lead to being too, er, self-absorbed—with career success, your social media image, or your spot on the leaderboard. Go left to find solace in a Source beyond your Self.

Take a Right

That said, an unhealthy preoccupation with Source may leave you detached from your health, socially isolated, or unrelatable and irresponsible. When you give yourself over completely to the divine without regard for your actions, thoughts, and emotions, you lose touch with your volition. In this case, migrate to the right to tune in to your embodied wisdom.

Life is a lot more fun when we move freely up and down and all around. Even though the ball is divided into quarters, it's one connected sphere with a globe's worth of vista points.

Now that you have a breakdown of existence to consider, what do you do, exactly, to establish a spiritual routine or build on one you've already got? The rest of this book will help with that. Each of the next four Tracks covers a different quadrant in detail. You'll get a good feel for the key aspects of each quarter of the Divine Disco Ball and a sense of how each operates. And you'll begin to see where and how you can connect with each cosmic corner.

That's where the Invites and Mystic Mixtapes come into, well, play. The Track for each quadrant contains an **Invite**, a step-by-step exercise for you to sample, designed to spark a deeper connection with IS. Delve into these when you're craving a stronger bond with your Self or Source.

For your everyday flicker, look to the seven activity suggestions listed in each Track's **Mystic Mixtape**. These short, sweet clips are winning ways to connect with your Self and Source on the regular; you get to choose if, which, when, where, how, and how often. Easy-peasy. With a simple yet superb way to dial into the Divine every day of the week, you'll be on your way to a regular spiritual practice in no time.

This four-quadrant framework serves as both an example and a potential anchor for DIY spirituality. There are endless ways to conceive of and create a meaningful system that works for you. Whether this serves as a landing pad or jumping-off place, the Divine Disco Ball is your DIY demo.

Infinite Source: The Divine Force

So what is Infinite Source, exactly? That's the trillion-dollar question. Are you thinking, "How much time you got?" It's kind of hard to capture the all-that-IS. Consider the mysterious, fabulous, mystabulous force that enlivens, informs, animates, and orchestrates this mind-bogglingly multifaceted life experience of yours. It's infinite in its reach, in its inclusion, and in its power. It's loving energy. In short, it's literally amazing.

IS cannot be fully understood. It's not for us humble human animals to comprehend IS. Our job is to celebrate IS.

We can't prove the existence of Infinite Source in a data collection kind of way. Yet, evidence shows up in subjective experience, and when it does, it's undeniable. Do you remember a time when you got a surefire hit that there's an unseen force at work in your life?

Maybe you felt it witnessing a birth, watching an eclipse, or glimpsing cosmic oneness on a psychedelic journey. Maybe you've cruised a wave of grace while painting for five hours straight or surfing at sunrise. Perhaps you were creating something innovative, like a musical arrangement or a new app, when you dropped into the zone. Or maybe you felt your Source in a moment of stillness, when you were doing nothing else. And how 'bout those mini miracles, like waking up at exactly the time you needed to, even though the alarm failed to go off? Or those definite hits from the universe that are totally random—message received? Bam.

If you've ever been touched by grace, no matter when or where it happened, you don't have to intellectualize it or justify it or defend it. It's sufficient to acknowledge it quietly to yourself—that unifying force that exists within us and all around us. Feel free to tip your hat to Infinite Source if you roll old school. When you're in the presence of the divine, everything feels fine. It just is.

We give so much credence to concrete, provable, scientifically validated reality. Science is indispensable and life-changingly incredible. But there is much more to life than what human intelligence—or even AI, for that matter—can grasp.

IS with You

No matter what type of rituals or traditions you embrace, you can enjoy a direct connection with Infinite Source, on demand. Connection is your birthright, and it's available from any age, at any time. One person doesn't have a more privileged relationship with IS than another—no VIP list, no premier-status line, no reservation required.

Just as we all have access to the air we breathe, we all have access to Infinite Source. How and when you relate with IS—indeed, *whether* you relate with IS—is up to you.

This means that in addition to, or independent of, an organized belief system, you can connect in your own unique way. How you go about connecting is entirely up to you. That is the basis of DIY spirituality. In an instant, you can tap into your connection with Infinite Source and be invigorated with a limitless supply of spiritual energy. You have easy access to the power that creates worlds. Wow!

Once you establish a connection to your Source, you'll never really be alone. Sure, you might enjoy or even crave the company of other people, and it's natural to feel lonely at times. We're social creatures, after all. But even in a moment of loneliness, if there's faith, then you're in good company. Now and always, you're loved completely, from your innermost core to every last cell in your body. You live in the glow of your originating life force. You cannot shine too brightly.

IS Your Origin

When your sense of permanent divine connection sinks in, you can let your significant others off the hook a little. It's normal to look to your people for fulfillment, love, and validation. But when you derive that essential sense of value from Infinite Source, you don't need to go looking for it in all the wrong places. Depending on other people for self-worth sets you up for disappointment. It's also not a fair thing to ask or expect. The good news is, unconditional love happens to be one of Infinite Source's superpowers.

You, yes you, have a cosmically perfect parent who loves you all the time, unconditionally. Indeed, there are the human beings who were responsible for getting you here and keeping you alive. But your true essence is from elsewhere. Your birth mom and dad influence your eye color, but your essential nature goes beyond the gene pool. Both you and IS are in charge of loving you like crazy, all the time, no matter what. Love showered upon you from other people is just rainbow sprinkles on the banana split. If you want ceaseless nurturing and constant adoration, you have two options: Give it to yourself, or soak it up from IS. If you do both, you've got it figured out.

The Meaning in the Mystery

What comes to mind for you when you think of the universe conspiring in your favor? Can you remember a time when bad news ended up being for the best, such as being laid off leading to a dream gig? Or getting dumped and subsequently meeting your better match? Divine redirection is not always delivered with a gentle touch. And yet, if you wait for the clarity of hindsight, you just might see how the universe was and is ever conspiring in your favor.

Much as you might like to take a shortcut to the happy ending, sometimes things have to get worse before they get better. It's not always easy to accept the curveballs you encounter. But what if you trust that your highest good is being served, or at least make space for the possibility that things will turn out to be for the best—whether or not you can see it? If at first this doesn't seem plausible, wait for it. Say someone accidentally rolls an overflowing grocery cart over your foot when you ran in just to buy an energy drink. And that guy turns out to play on your favorite pro hockey team and insists you take his ice-side seats at the next home game. Quite the cool collision. Sometimes, the meaning in the mystery is revealed later. Stay on the lookout.

Then again, there are times when stuff will never make sense. Shit happens, and unfortunately, tragedy does too. Shitty shitstorm exceptions aside, pretty often, the tough stuff comes with a payoff—often a life-altering lesson. Like it or not, detours play an important part in your destiny.

Sometimes, we get to coast along in the flow. The right things unfold in divine timing. When life goes your way and you get a seemingly magical result, consider all the minute factors that came into play to support you. Gratitude is in order. Thank your lucky stars and your generous Infinite Source.

Miracles happen. Mysteries abound. Might as well delight in divine intervention. It's so much fun to live in a sustained state of awe. When you open to a spiritual influence, a new level of *all good* is available to you. It's a relief to know you don't have to do life on your own. Notice the divine winks. Look for hints that there is an unseen influence lighting your way. Ask IS to send a sign. Suss out the meaning in the mystery.

Collaborating with IS

Once convinced that *yeah, Infinite Source is playing along*, you might as well enlist IS for help. Leveraging your cosmic creative partner is like adding rocket fuel to your aspirations. Of course, you can't expect IS to do all the heavy lifting. You don't even get to choose specifically how, when, and where the support, sponsored by grace, is going to show up. The best you can do is ask for spiritual guidance and then get to work— baby step by tedious little baby step.

Yes, you actually have to do things. But doing the things is a lot easier with otherwordly wind beneath your wings. Free will is your part and your power. However, when your will and divine will are one, you are aligned, lit, and primed. If you want to cocreate with IS, include IS in your plans. A simple formula is to set an intention, ask IS for an assist, and haul ass toward your desires. Even so, be mindful of what you're signing up for. Some dreams aren't meant to come true as you'd envisioned. Keep at it long enough to see what comes of the creative collaboration between you and IS.

If it's in the flow, you'll know. If not, it was an important stop along the way to what the universe has in store for you, which is bound to be even better. Keep in mind, this life thingy is a cocreation. You and your Source partner perfectly to get things done.

Make Work Work for You

Modern hustle culture has brainwashed people to believe that the harder they grind, the better the result will be. There is some truth to that. In the words of RuPaul, *you better work*. But it's possible to labor too hard. Then the process ceases to be a soulful collab and becomes a draining drag. Even worse, if your sneaky ego takes charge, the once fun endeavor may devolve into a competition with other people doing similar things. It feels like a struggle because it is. That's where faith can swoop in and save the show.

Remembering to trust that everything is unfolding as it should, you simply step forward persistently in the direction of your dreams while surrendering the outcome to IS. As the grand conductor, IS has infinite storage space for what lies in and well beyond your most optimistic imagination. So dream big.

It's useful to become comfortable with uncertainty, because whether or not you consciously surrender, you can't always be in control. The unknown is inevitable. Uncertainty is a constant.

So what's it going to be? Anxiety? Or awe?

How about curiosity? This is quite an unfolding, eh? Reassured that it's not all up to you, you can feel relieved, connected, and even more motivated. Remember: *Surrender doesn't mean giving up; it means letting go.* So when you've put forth your wish, formulated a solid plan, done your part, and surrendered the rest to Infinite Source, say to yourself, "IS in charge."

Invite: Link Up

How about getting into the habit of noticing, appreciating, and celebrating your Source?
Let's replay your own personal IS soundtrack. Grab a notepad and find a comfortable place to chill and contemplate.

1. Reflect on divine interventions. Think back to times in your life that can only be explained by the universe conspiring in your favor. Maybe it was how you met your BFF or how you narrowly escaped an accident. Maybe it was when you took a wrong turn and ended up making a lucky discovery. In hindsight, what seems meant to be?

2. Be awe-inspired. Can you feel the goosebumps as you appreciate the divine wisdom that informed the unfolding captured in your memories? Accept these IS imprints as evidence of eternal love and support from your adoring, silent partner. Realize you received the divine assist. You don't have to dismiss it, downplay it, or second-guess it. It just is.

3. Feel supported. IS was and is with you. That means you don't have to do life solo. You're accompanied and supported constantly. Sit with this feeling of being held and uplifted by IS for a moment. Then write about what it feels like to know you are part of IS and IS is part of you.

4. Identify missed connections. IS is sending you messages all the time; you just need to be open to receiving them. Maybe your motivation music kept playing at random, but you chalked it up to coincidence, or just the right bit of info came into your life to help you with a decision at just the right time. Jot down what you notice looking back through lit lenses.

5. Start noticing, appreciating, and celebrating IS. Commit to a habit of noticing when things are in sync. You can start this very moment. Press pause and look around. Is there anything that captures your attention as, like, awe-mazing? Things clicking into place? A blessing dressed up like a setback? When you stumble on a sign of IS in effect, appreciate it. Like, *Damn, this is so cool. Thanks, IS*. Doesn't it kind of make you want to celebrate? Let that spark grow into a flame and dance it out.

MYSTIC MIXTAPE
FOR INFINITE SOURCE

WINNING WAYS TO CONNECT WITH IS DAILY

Tune In

Although it's possible to connect with IS anytime, anywhere, the relationship thrives on your focus. Pick a cue to remind you to connect. You might adopt a popular spiritually significant time, like 11:11 a.m. and p.m., to establish the habit. Or dabble in sacred geometry's intriguing take on numbers: 3 for balance, 6 for harmony, 7 for divine order, and 9 for enlightenment.

Whenever your magic number hits you, a simple shout-out to IS does the job. Include any divine beings in your circle—guardian angel, spiritual guide, fave deity, spirit animal, or ancestor—as often as you like. You can say, "Hola, IS!" Or go further: "I ask you to be with me. I give you permission to be with me. And I thank you for being with me."

DM IS

When you have a decision to make, an obstacle to overcome, or just want a little spiritual help, simply ask IS for guidance. You don't need your phone to direct message IS. Do it the old-fashioned way: spoken in a prayer or a song, or written down in your journal.

You can throw out *Can I get a little help here?* Make your plea silently to yourself or out loud, ask as you begin or end a meditation session—whatever feels right to you. Then thank Infinite Source for the divine assist that's already on the way.

Mark the Mini Miracles

Miracles big and small are happening all the time. The key is to acknowledge them. Track them, even. An assist may show up in the next text message you receive, sunset you watch, or errand you run. Stay awake to the wonder.

Every day, count a miracle for each of your fingers. Just rattle off ten mini (or major) miracles: *The dog saw the vet just in time; I pulled right up to a perfect parking spot; my FedEx package came just as I was walking out.* If you're really present to all that's occurring with you and for you, you just might be smiling for most of your day. You'll begin to see that marking miracles brings about more miracles. How wild is that?

Wait for It

When we take a leap of faith that the universe is conspiring in our favor, we can eventually see how maybe a closed door leads to a better opportunity. It takes patience and faith, but once IS has earned your trust, you can let go of those daily Debbie Downer doubts.

The next time there's a mishap, make some space for the possibility that everything is unfolding as it should. As the Stoics observed, the obstacle is the way. Let go of the need to control an outcome. Chuckle when a curveball falls in your lap, knowing IS has a plan. Sometimes the biggest hits start with scratches on the record.

Rest in the Rhythm

You don't have to read sheet music to know that there are rests between notes. The pauses are just as important to a good melody as the sounds. This logic applies to your life and in creating closeness to IS: Find balance between action and rest, between chaos and calm.

You are a human being, not a human doing. So settle down, already. IS isn't impressed with your to-do list. IS wants your company in the quiet moments, when you can be fully present in the spaces between breaths, beats, goals, and gab. In the stillness, you will find IS. Create that space. Shhhhh. Step off the treadmill once in a while and attune to Source in the sound of silence.

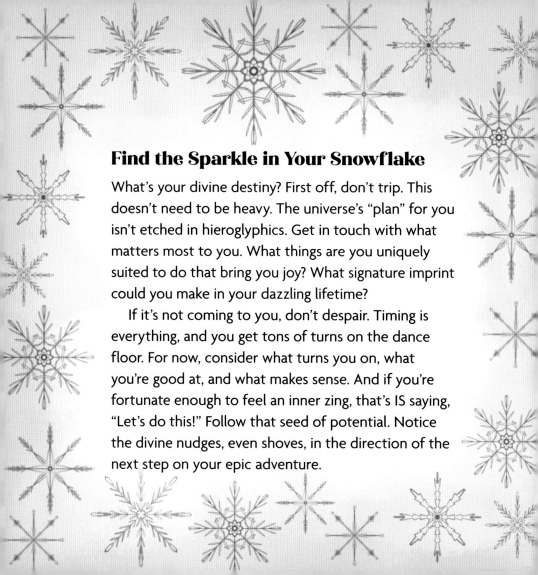

Find the Sparkle in Your Snowflake

What's your divine destiny? First off, don't trip. This doesn't need to be heavy. The universe's "plan" for you isn't etched in hieroglyphics. Get in touch with what matters most to you. What things are you uniquely suited to do that bring you joy? What signature imprint could you make in your dazzling lifetime?

If it's not coming to you, don't despair. Timing is everything, and you get tons of turns on the dance floor. For now, consider what turns you on, what you're good at, and what makes sense. And if you're fortunate enough to feel an inner zing, that's IS saying, "Let's do this!" Follow that seed of potential. Notice the divine nudges, even shoves, in the direction of the next step on your epic adventure.

Be Beyond Your Brain

With all the flips your mind can do on any given day, it's easy to forget that IS is with you. One way to keep IS on your radar is with a visual touchstone. Pick a symbol or let a symbol pick you. Make it a meaningful icon—like a feather or a flame, a gem or a crystal, the tree whose branches wave outside your window, an altar, a statuette, a sacred tattoo, the Divine Disco Ball. . . .

Let your chosen symbol anchor you to the transcendent truth that lies beyond the random meanderings of imperfect and sometimes unhelpful brain patterns. Find comfort and peace in your current symbol for IS, amidst any chaos.

Infinite Self:
The Divine in You

Even if you don't fully buy the idea of a divine source out there, perhaps you have a sure sense that there's a pure, sacred, celestial spark within you. *Ring, ring!* That sweet rich center could be called consciousness, Atman, inner wisdom, soul, spirit, essence, higher self, or Bobby McGee. Your DIY DJ might like Infinite Self. Go with whatever suits it, because that perfect part of you knows what's up.

The Infinite Self encompasses love, life force, inspiration, and spiritual truth. In action, it shows itself as immaculate intuition, sage wisdom, profound peace, and spontaneous joy. It may be underestimated because it's invisible to the eye; however, it's seriously there and legit badass. Your Infinite Self is the pearl in your oyster, the yolk in your egg, the flame of your candle. It's precious. It's central. It's the true-blue you.

Oblivious though we may be of its presence, Infinite Self does call attention to itself sometimes. In those vibey moments, your inner divinity cannot be denied. You trust yourself. You choose love. You forgive because it feels good. You find compassion. You take the high road. You smile effortlessly as an expression of your open heart. You're connected to IS. You're guided. You're aligned. You can't stop the feeling.

On random and clarity-inducing occasions, you may spontaneously get a hit from your Infinite Self. What does that feel like? An epiphany. An insight. A brainstorm. A directive. Connectedness. Certainty. Human potential tapped. Transcendence of all things petty and ego-driven.

Have you ever felt super elevated, optimistic, and effervescent? Yes? It's like you're floating on champagne bubbles, yet your poolside brunch mimosa was virgin. How do you account for your bliss? A certain euphoric energy arises from within you, and it feels good. That's the fiery furnace of your sacred flame all lit up.

You get the general idea. So . . . what if it's been a while since you said "hey" to your spirit-soul-sparky-inner-wisdom part? No problem. It's still there. You don't have to wait for a solar bulb in you to suddenly switch on to be connected to your Infinite Self. Turn on the bright lights with a flick of faith.

Employing Your Observer

Like the sea, the depths of your emotional, spiritual, intellectual, and psychological being don't show on the surface. It takes a deep dive to get there, and few will ever be invited. Maybe you will allow someone in: a best friend, a partner, a parent, a therapist, or your podcast audience of thousands. What goes on under the surface of you is miraculous. How deep you go and who you share your sunken treasure with is entirely up to you. There's always more of you to discover.

If you're looking for your inner wisdom, employ your "Observer." This is the transcendent part of you that watches everything go down. Your silent witness, it notices without judgment your thoughts, feelings, and behaviors, without becoming entangled in them. Can you recall a time when you said or did something while simultaneously being aware of it on another level? Totally trippy in a good way, right? Your Observer is always there. Yet, being conscious of it can happen with intention or at random times, like déjà vu.

Maybe you're able to take a sec right now to zoom out and see yourself reading this book from a higher vantage point, yes? We all have this Observer part as an aspect of our existence. It's a wonderful ally. Finding your Observer before you speak or act, at times, may slow you down just enough to save yourself from a major oops. It's also there to teach equanimity—the ability to stay detached whether an experience is negative, positive, or neutral. It's with you right now; can you find it? This wise, intangible aspect of yourself is indispensable and largely underutilized. Hello.

If you can locate your Observer, you're tapping into your spiritual nature. Make friends with it and it will serve you well.

Engaging Your Immaculate Intuition

When you're dealing with a dilemma, your mind likely spins into an intellectual deliberation. You end up overthinking and overcontrolling in an effort to find the best solution. Yes, your mind evolved to focus on what's wrong to keep you alive, but the brain can only come up with so many solutions before analysis-paralysis sets in. This is where Infinite Self can save the day. Go deeply inward and find your unshakable intuitive anchor. The right choice makes itself known when you get still and tune in to your embodied wisdom. Collect data from Infinite Self before you make the call. It's more reliable than ChatGPT.

Skeptical? Think back to an experience you've had in which you internally sensed what was true for you. People often describe this as a "gut feeling." Or they might say, "I just knew it!" These experiences radiate the answers found in your Infinite Self: that sacred part of you that's as divine as Infinite Source. False modesty aside, you know you're a total rock star at the core, right?

Cosmic Chills

Ever get the funny feeling you're being stared at, only to find that when you turn around, you're right? There's something unaccounted for at work here, unless you have eyeballs in the back of your head. We're one, not just with other living things, but also with consciousness and the cosmos. It's freaky, and we like it. If you have a dream that foretells the future, don't chalk it up to crazy. Recognize the cosmic fabric you're threaded into.

Much can be said about the interconnectedness of existence. Contemplate for a sec, if you will, how far-reaching your connectedness really is. Take the cool and uncanny example of quantum entanglement. When a pair of entangled particles is separated, they maintain their relative states, such as spin or polarity, even when they're miles apart. Change one particle's state, and the other changes simultaneously. Scientists observing these effects believe the same thing would happen even if the particles were located across the universe. How can two particles be connected when they're miles or light-years apart? It's not on the quiz—just another glimpse of the invisible web woven by Infinite Source. Whether you're talkin' spooky action at a distance or everyday karma, you and your impact are part of the cosmic mashup.

This stuff may be written off as weird, which makes total sense, but it's as real as anything else. You could feel embarrassment, shame, or fear about your mysterious experiences. But don't. Be curious. Be in awe.

Indeed, we all have the capacity to access hidden aspects of consciousness. Plenty of people have foreseen events, from *I had a feeling this would happen* or *Whoa—I totally saw that coming* to a full-on psychic premonition. And all of us have had those unbelievable experiences that were inexplicably in sync. We're elegantly included in the intricate orchestration of all that IS.

You're not just made up of matter—you matter. In fact, you're a shining star, made of stardust. Billions of years ago, stars created elements that are essential to all of life, including you! When stars explode into a supernova, basically the biggest fireworks show ever, they scatter themselves like glitter in space. These star seeds become the basis for new things: fresh stars, planets, moons, and life on Earth. So yes, you are literally a cosmic creature originating from stars. This gives new meaning to the idea of star power.

Spiritual Connections

No matter how close or distant you are to your fellow shining stars, you are inseparable. Like a facet on the Divine Disco Ball, you are one brilliant piece and also part of something bigger and brighter.

Your Infinite Self can dial into the Infinite Self of others, and vice versa. Ever met someone and had an instant connection—like you *knew* them already (*Have we met?*) or had an uncanny desire to get to know them for reasons you can't explain? Then you've experienced the invisible electrical current and binding force that can bring strangers together. Go ahead and let that interaction run its course—whether for a convo, a coffee, or coupledom.

Tapping into your Infinite Self to interpret encounters with others can help you read people and situations. For example, when you pick up on someone else's antisocial signal—or they pick up on yours—it might just be a quick read of whether they are giving off warm and welcoming nonverbal signals of interest, or something that feels more closed off and aloof. Don't take it personally. We all have days when we aren't really up for mixing it up. If you have ever felt like an exposed nerve out in public, you can empathize with someone else's need to hide under a hoodie. It's okay. The point is, you are sending and receiving energetic signals, and this is a viable form of communication.

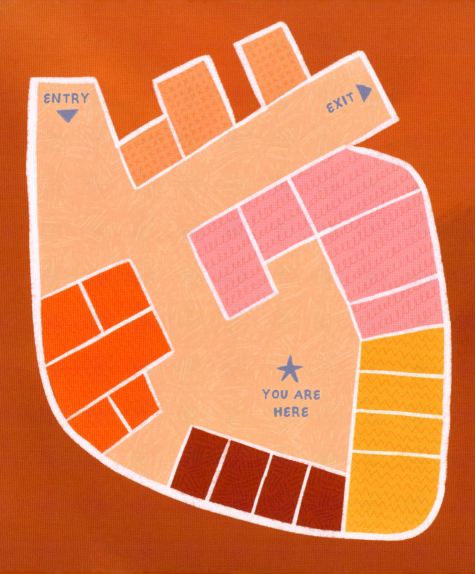

Shine Love and Light

So how do you vibe out positive energy? Try transmitting love and light. Maybe take a page from the yogi playbook. In the spirit of *namaste*—a Sanskrit word meaning "I bow to the divine within you" and spoken typically at the end of yoga class—you can honor another by saluting the spiritual essence in us all. Basically, you're saying "My inner spark acknowledges your inner spark" or "Real recognizes real."

If a connection is meant to be, you will feel engaged, warm, and comfortable after the initial awkwardness wears off. If you simply allow for the possibility that there may be divine intervention at work, down to the level of who you find yourself sitting next to in a college auditorium, then you're acknowledging a link to others and to IS. You can have an open heart without being an energy sponge.

On the other hand, if your Spidey sense tells you to go the other way—trust that. This is your intuition telling you that this interaction isn't meant for you. Don't be too passive to internally discern, *Thank you, next.*

If loving thy neighbor seems like a stretch, just allow for the fact that they have an Infinite Self too—no matter how deeply buried. You can be your best self and meet someone else's worst self. Even if it doesn't seem like your good energy lands in the moment, your neighbor may catch up. In any case, you'll do no harm, even if you dislike the a-hole. Then, you're free to go your separate ways—or out for pizza, as the case may be.

Truth is, everyone has those off moments, and everyone includes you. Ever been hangry? Lost a night of sleep and become a nightmare to all who crossed your path the next morning? It's normal to be the problem every once in a while. Remember: Be kind to yourself through it, and you will recover your sense of humor and gain a more positive outlook.

That positivity can be infectious, so watch out! You just might shoot amorous arrows into the heart of your next fling or forever mate. When you have feelings for someone, take a chance and be vulnerable. Leading with your heart means you risk rejection. Yet rejection in life is inevitable. So follow up on your crush—deeply, fearlessly. Be bold, because love is a divine gift to be savored.

Invite: Turn It Up

So how do you get anchored in your Infinite Self? You may have a fast track for this. But here's a scenic route to light your way.

1. Listen. Remain open to receiving the divine download. Think of your Infinite Self as a satellite dish, receiving input from Infinite Source. Listen for messages. Notice hints. Take in signs of all kinds. Close your eyes and sink into your heart on the waves of your breath. Now you're open and clear to receive messages from the spiritual realm.

2. Feel. Don't be surprised if strong emotions arise during these sacred times. Pay close attention to them, because those feelings are the voice of your Infinite Self—the divinely perfect part of you. What you *think* takes center stage most of the time, so it's important to get a read on what you *feel* to get the whole picture. Put your brain on airplane mode and allow your feelings the luxury of space. Truly tune in to your core. Don't be afraid to search out your feelings, shed a tear, or laugh to yourself. This step isn't about figuring it out; it's about *feeling it out*.

3. Fact-check. To some extent, history, wounds, well-worn patterns, and trauma stick with you as a cautionary tale and as a filter for danger. It's natural—this is your body-mind protecting your precious essence. Therefore, discernment is a must. Be sure to investigate any worrisome thoughts, knee-jerk reactions, or funky signals worth questioning. Be your own detective. What is your inner world trying to tell you? Ask, *What do you want me to know? What was that about? What do I need to do or not do?* Chill for a while and then decide. The key is remembering that *just because you have a feeling, thought, sensation, or memory doesn't mean it must be acted upon.*

4. Follow. Once you've received what arises from taking a dedicated listen and had some time to assimilate, you can reflect and consider what to do with it, if anything. Ask yourself, *What's in alignment with my inner wisdom?* This is where your thinking becomes most useful, by helping yourself determine a precise plan of action. Allow your head to handle the tactics as you move in alignment with your feelings, led by your inner wisdom—your truth, your intuition. Be willing to fearlessly head in that direction. As you attune to what's true for you and follow where that leads, miraculous events occur.

MYSTIC MIXTAPE FOR INFINITE SELF

winning ways to connect with **IS** daily

Go on a Phone Fast

OMG, get off your phone and come back to your soul! The smartphone is the gadget that fills in all the blank space. It's like that annoying relative who talks too much just to make sure there's no break in conversation. We tell ourselves that me-time with screentime is our special downtime. But how can that be if scrolling is making you anxious, jealous, or lonely? Give your sweet innocent essence a break and unplug. Choose your challenge: Go without your phone for one hour each day, or one day a week. Or limit yourself to emails, texts, and calls, but cut out all social media. You might find that your Infinite Self is plenty entertaining itself.

Celebrate Right Now

Take a deep breath and observe what's going on now. There's no need to judge. Just notice. What sounds are you aware of? A ceiling fan? A muffled conversation? What's going on physically right now? Are you clenching your teeth? Squinting your eyes? Cut it out. Relax.

Run through all your senses and see what's up. Any smells? How's the temperature? Are you getting caught up in a million problems or big emotions? Can you call on your Observer to acknowledge your thoughts and feelings without responding to them? Life continues when you are reviewing the past or planning for the future. So snap out of time travel and sink into the now. Notice life happening in each moment.

Better Be Good to the Greatest Love of All

No matter your situation, your past, your birthstone, or what you had for breakfast, you deserve your adoration. Think of yourself as containing every age you've ever been, like the rings of a tree trunk mark each year. Your younger selves are still with you, and sometimes they cry out for the comfort of your company.

Recognize that you need compassion. Don't criticize. Offer yourself what you need deep down. A pep talk? A pat on the back for small chores and good behavior? Some simple self-kindness? Love your Infinite Self as Infinite Source loves you. Start saying, "Okayyy, legend!" to yourself 10+ times a day.

Dance with Yourself

One way to clean house and get reacquainted with your Infinite Self is to take a time-out, just to be with me, myself, and I. Go away for a spell. Or do a staycation. Do so as often as you need it and without apology. Maybe you sneak off to a concert all by yourself, or get an Airbnb for a solo weekend in the country.

Remind yourself that you're taking a healthy, much-needed step toward enjoying your own company. For some people, being alone feels a little scary at first. Because, yes, you will begin to know thyself. In time, you may begin to like—even insist upon—your sweet moments of alone time to achieve overall balance.

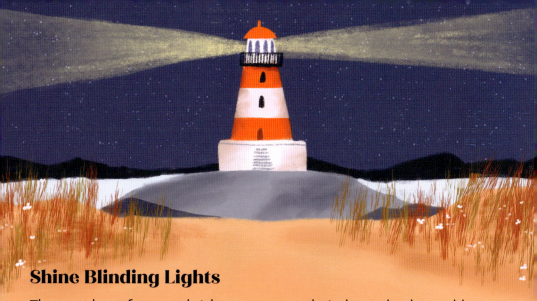

Shine Blinding Lights

There are lots of ways to brighten someone else's day, make the world a better place, and improve a situation. Imagine you are a lighthouse in a dark and stormy harbor. The boats know how to find the shore because there's a ray of luminous light beaming out so brightly that it's unmistakable. What a relief for those ships lost at sea! Think about the effect you can have on lost souls. You don't have to say anything. Just turn on your heartlight. It's healing for people to be in your presence when your Infinite Self radiates from the inside out. Embody love, light, and joy, and experiment with the reactions you get. Warning: Your light shining brightly is irresistibly attractive, so be prepared for some looks, hottie.

Score a One-Hit Wonder

You come across people every day you hardly take notice of. Time to pump up the volume. A single interaction, no matter how brief, can be mood boosting on both sides. So instead of downplaying a pass in the hallway, play the one-hit wonder game.

Before you encounter a stranger in an elevator or in line at the supermarket, take a quick inventory of your mood. If 1 is dead and 10 is euphoric, what's your state on the scale? Then, go ahead, strike up a light-hearted banter, give a compliment, or tell a joke. Afterward, revisit the scale. Did you get a dopamine boost? Does it seem like they did too? See how many times you can score a one-hit wonder in a day. Then beat your streak tomorrow.

Harmonize Your Energy

One easy point of entry to engage your spiritual nature is to learn the seven main chakras and get in touch with each of them daily. Found from the base of your spine to the crown of your head, each of these energy centers represents a vital function. Once you balance your chakras, you will be firing on all cylinders and spiritually stacked for what's to come. Here's a just a snippet:

	Chakra	Meaning	Inner Anthem
	Crown of head	Connection to IS, truth, consciousness	I'm tuned in
	Third Eye	Intuition, sight and perception	I see
	Throat	Communication, speaking your truth, authenticity	I'm voicing
	Heart	Compassion, love, kindness	I love
	Solar plexus	Will, confidence, power	I'm on it
	Sacral	Creativity, emotions, pleasure	I feel
	Root	Stability, vitality, security	I'm solid

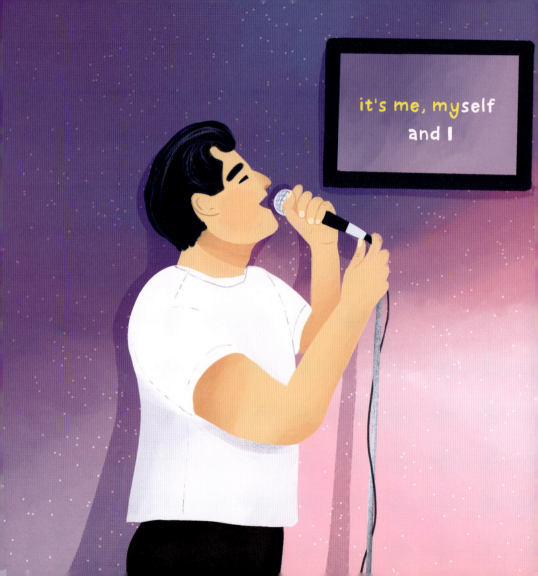

Incarnate Self: The Divine in the Flesh

Let's turn the spotlight on your beautiful body and bright mind. Your Incarnate Self encompasses your fabulous, fascinating physical *and* mental functions. In this quarter of the Divine Disco Ball, we're talking about the stuff that makes you human—not a totally bad species to be, if you can't be a dolphin.

Your body and mind work together to keep you humming in real life. In fact, you couldn't hum, much less sing, without the coordination of your entire being. From your grounded feet to your resonating head, your vessel generates, vibrates, and projects sound. Your heart and soul imbue your voice with feeling, while your mind orchestrates the notes and learns the lyrics. Computer culture gives mental capacity disproportionate emphasis. You aren't just a gelatinous gray brain; you are a whole instrument.

Tending the Temple

It's an act of reverence to take care of your whole self, in every sense. When it comes to your physical form, you gotta tend the temple. Your body sets the stage for your soul and spirit. Bridging the nonphysical realm (Infinite Self) to the tangible turf of form is what your Incarnate Self is all about.

Your physical self does the acting, drumming, and dancing, and your mind is the director, conductor, and choreographer. Both are necessary for your true self to perform. And if you incorporate your Infinite Self into the act, you're a superstar.

You could say your Incarnate Self is your personal shrine to the divine. We regard our spiritual spaces—from altar to labyrinth, temple to church, mountain to vortex—as sacred. Your Incarnate Self is no different. What's deep within your amazing body and mind is pure, precious, and transcendent. The hardware and operating system that house your Infinite Self deserve your protection, nurturing, honor, adoration, and basic maintenance.

Indeed, without your regular attention, your total package would cease to exist. Good self-care can look like flossing your pearly whites to flash that sexy smile, showering a bad day off your skin, sleeping plenty to function better awake, and fueling your machine with what keeps it operationally optimal. The daily stuff you do makes or breaks your health. All those seemingly minor decisions add up to have a major impact. Without health, you die. Put another way, everything you're fond of—be it thin-crust pizza, playing catch with your Rhodesian Ridgeback, rolling between the sheets, scrolling for funny videos, a concert at Red Rocks, or a Red Sox game—isn't so fun anymore without a strong body and mind.

Keeping It Fresh

Think of your body as your boombox. It's the machine that plays your music. Nothing can happen if it's broken. So make sure it runs smoothly. The moment you power up for the day, you can begin attuning to the intention to have an epic one. If you aren't a morning person, do it whenever, but heed this: No matter what time you crack your lids, do so with the perspective that this is the first day of the rest of your life.

Your physical body must move you through your day, so make your actions count. As a suggestion, start with a drink of water—warm or room temperature—to clean out the pipes. Keep hydrated all day. Breathe fresh air and inhale deeply. Eat things that are good for you most of the time.

Move through your day with presence and gratitude for blessings and miracles, and cocreate your own. Follow your dreams, but be practical. Use what your mama gave you and do the things—and then for god/dess sakes, relax. Go to sleep with appreciation for a night of rest without demands. Rinse. Repeat.

For the official instruction manual on how to be an embodied human being, contact customer service at 1-800-ADULTING, or scan the QR code provided.

Start Me Up

What you eat has a huge impact on you. So get reacquainted with your old friends fruits and veggies. Find ways to prepare them that make them delicious. Look to living foods straight from Incarnate Source to add vibrancy to your vessel and glow to your skin.

Your body actually has a way of craving what it needs—science calls this *intuitive eating*. While the USDA provides guidelines for healthy eating, countless experts say that one-size-fits-all approaches simply cannot meet the unique needs of our unique constitutions. *Okay, then.* So how do you know what's "healthy" for you? Ask your body! When you can pause and connect with the wisdom of your flesh, you may sense a craving for bananas and later realize that your muscles yearned for the repair expedited by potassium. If you're craving ice cream, no judgment. Maybe just look inward to see if that's truly what you desire, or if, in fact, you need a hug.

Feeding your Incarnate Self intuitively is a form of self-preservation, self-love and, well, just giving a rat's ass about your incredible package. Drive-through detours are okay occasionally—but do your best to choose clean eats your body needs to thrive over mystery ingredients that make you sluggish, or worse, sick.

Aside from *what* you eat, consider when, where, and how. Unless you have the graveyard shift, don't grab a bag of chips at 1:23 a.m. and munch through it on the couch in front of the show you're bingeing. This is no bueno, mi amigo. Food is fuel. You need it throughout the day, not right before bed when you're powering down for a solid night's rest.

To be more conscious of what and when you eat, consider making one meal a day sacred. Slow your roll as you bite down, chew, savor, and swallow. Your taste buds will thank you when you make time for an intentional, mindful feast.

Beyond curating good culinary customs, be choosy about input of every kind—not just food and drink, but also what you hear, read, watch, and pick up from other people. Be conscious of what honors you and

what doesn't. In appreciation for yourself and your Source, stay aware of everything you ingest, from goat cheese to gossip. Only take in quality fuel on all fronts. Keep your food pure, your thoughts constructive, and your friends true. Love yourself too much to settle for anything that brings you down.

Mind-Body Collab

Your life force—that big energy byproduct of good nutrition, sleep, exercise, and outlook—is one thing. Your vibration is another. You know when you're giving and getting good vibes, right? Like the resonance of plucked guitar strings, those signals ripple outward. Your inner state informs your outer aura. You are responsible for the energy you emit, so do us all a favor and light up the dance floor.

If that feels a little woo-woo, consider more sciencey stuff. Like how the gut-brain axis allows two-way communication between your nervous system and gastrointestinal system. Believe it or not, your gut bacteria can affect how well you think and how good you feel. Likewise, the heart sends signals to the brain that affect emotion regulation, decision-making, and stress responses. If this still feels a little hard to grasp, maybe all you need is a better sense of humor. Believe it or not, cracking up actually helps you get cracking. Because the physical act of laughter reduces stress hormones like cortisol and releases feel-good endorphins, which can refresh your mind and make it easier to focus and be productive. Not even kidding.

Express Yourself

It's time to reveal the real you through some next-level swag. Celebrate your inner spark by flaunting who you are on the outside. Your Incarnate Self is the neon sign that signifies the brilliant being you are at the core. You get to design that sign. You decide what it looks like and what it says, because you know you best. Hair is just a skull shield until the cut shouts "niiiiiice." Shoes are just buffers from the sidewalk until you make 'em a shrine for your bouncing feet. So get thee to thy local thrift shop and show up like you mean it.

If fashion isn't your mode of self-expression, maybe you have a tattoo flirtatiously placed on your body that sums you up, only for those who get it. Or some bling that hints at where you come from. It takes effort to be a walking work of art day to day, but when the mood strikes, show off who you really are from the inside out. Wear what resonates, let your inner truth be your only real influencer, strut your stuff, and prepare to get looks. That's a sign that you are inspiring.

PS: Thank you for looking so you.

No Judgment

Permission to be yourself is ironically given to you from yourself. Are you doing it? Other people have a way of conning you into conformity, but whether you cop to that or not is your choice. Just remember what Oscar Wilde and others have said, "Be yourself; everyone else is already taken."

Your chosen people, tribe, and partners will love you more the more they know the real you. That's what makes you intriguing, unique, and refreshing. However: Don't expect everyone to like you or get you.

Rejection is an inevitable experience that everyone encounters. Not only that, rejection is Source's protection. If someone isn't all about you, they aren't aligned with your highest good. Trust that.

Your people shall hopefully do their best to honor thy pronouns, whether she/he/they do so clumsily or with grace. Give the old folks a break here. They gotta get used to new norms just like their elders got used to texting. Eventually, they will catch up with the times, thanks to neuroplasticity. If not, well, you can offer compassion or forgiveness, or simply strike a tolerant pose. No point in sinking to their level and judging the judger. Rise above it, bro.

What matters is that you get to live your authentic truth. That goes for all the things, in addition to spirituality—including sexual orientation, gender identity, neurodiversity, cultural background, body positivity, and musical taste. You might consider yourself fluid rather than fixed, or private rather than public. It's all part of your choice to express yourself. Spin it your way—it's so you, and that's how we like it!

Invite: Mental Pause

Meditation is an easy way to take a pause and soothe your soul. At its core, meditating is simply being quiet, noticing, and letting go. And research shows any amount of meditation, even a few minutes, does your mind-body health a solid. To find your groove, try out this breath-focused meditation, or sample some meditation apps and videos.

1. Pick a place. Choose a spot where you're unlikely to be interrupted. Grab whatever you need: chair, yoga mat, pillow, or patch of grass.

2. Set a timer. Consider what you can afford—5, 12, 20 minutes— whatever feels doable. Then use a timer, a watch, or an app that dings when time is up. If you can silence your phone otherwise, do so.

3. Sit in a comfortable position. Keep your back straight yet relaxed. Aim for a reverant but not rigid posture. Close your eyes. Rest your hands on your lap, knees, or thighs with palms open and facing up to receive or down to get grounded.

4. Breathe deeply. Focus on each inhale, each exhale, and the spaces between. Sink into the present moment. Your breath is home base, so come back to it, again and again, with your mindful attention.

5. Notice body sensations. Attend to any physical discomfort without judgment. If you have a tight jaw, for example, release that tightness with compassion for your stressed-out self.

6. Let it be. Stay the detached observer of your thinking mind and your feeling body. Allow thoughts to come and go without letting them hijack your attention.

7. Return to the breath. If you catch yourself evaluating your meditation while you're doing it, that's normal. Spinning out solving a problem? No problem. Return to the breath. More thoughts? Go back to your breath.

8. Go on with your day. Eventually you will get the ding that you're done. Then find your feet and go do your thing. Stay open to benefits and subtle shifts that may sneak up on you over time if you continue to practice meditation.

MYSTIC MIXTAPE FOR INCARNATE SELF

WINNING WAYS TO CONNECT WITH IS DAILY

A

MIXTAPE #3

Get on the Floor

Your dancing feet aren't just fun to watch, they're doing you a solid. You already know that exercise promotes long life, happiness, strength, and vitality, but did you know it can be a spiritual act, too? If you make movement a ritual of appreciation for your incredible Incarnate Self, it becomes a spiritual practice. Whether you're walking, swimming, snowboarding, lifting weights, or sweating through a Pilates class, consider the activity a sacred act of reverence. Set aside some time each day just for fitness—20 minutes, an hour, or whatever you can get away with. Regular exercise is an expression of love of life in motion. Good times.

Make Your Mind a Nice Place to Be

Your brain automatically generates thoughts 24/7. Yet the quality of those thoughts is random, unless you intervene. A typical mind tends toward problems, stressing about the past and worrying about the future. That's valid, but it sucks. Your mind is hypervigilant because you might be attacked by a cave hyena even though you no longer live in the Stone Age.

The trick is to redirect your attention to something useful—the current moment, for starters. Mindfulness is a go-to tool to help you focus on what really matters, which is what's happening right now. Try replacing unhelpful thoughts with those grounded in conscious presence. Don't let your brain be the boss of you. It's your avatar, not your player.

Befriend Your Incarnate Self

Your body and mind deserve your adoration. Get in the habit of sending messages of appreciation. The next time you stub your toe, instead of cursing it for running into the table leg, thank your ten toes for being so dependable all the time. Thank your brain when you ace a test. Thank your reflexes when you avert a collision. Thank your leg muscles when you finish a marathon. Appreciate the vast network of organs and enzymes that digest every meal. You only have one body in this life, so express gratitude for it.

Know Your Parts

How well do you know yourself? Psychotherapy, including "parts work," can help unravel your hidden mysteries, if you're curious. And you can investigate on your own.

For fun, try this: Observe aspects of yourself and name the different parts you discover. For example, you may find Inner Critic Ivan, Guilt Trip Glenda, Arrogant Angie, or Pleaser Pedro. Everyone has myriad parts, all with important functions. Even the ones you might not like are there to help you in some way. They have roles to play, but they don't all need to be center stage at once. Get to know your cast. Dialogue with them on paper. Sketch your favorite characters on a poster. Maybe you'll choose to put a new part of you in the limelight for a while. How 'bout your soul?

Bounce Back

Accept that there will be challenges, setbacks, and slipups. Yep, bad days happen. This is totally normal. Predictable, even. Struggle is the reason success is sweet. Bounce back with resilience and keep going. Dr. K says, "Confidence doesn't come from success. It comes from surviving failure." See failure as a growth opportunity and crisis as a step on the way to transformation. Joseph Campbell's definition of the hero's journey includes the "Abyss" stage, which is demonstrated in epic sagas like Star Wars and Harry Potter.

In spiritual terms, before you become enlightened, you may encounter a dark night of the soul. So, although it's no fun at the time, see hardship as a sign that you're getting somewhere. Enlist IS for reinforcements, and keep the faith. No matter what, keep going. The only way is through.

Dream On

Your mind and emotions need to process all that you put yourself through in the waking state. This happens during shut-eye, so think of your bed as the charging station for your Incarnate Self. Consider your sleep hygiene, because it affects the whole twenty-four hours. Your body digs a regular beat, so create a supportive ritual for your rest. If you're on screens within two hours of your head hitting the pillow, you're more likely to have trouble falling asleep, because the blue light from your devices can seriously mess with your body's circadian rhythm. Aim for the same bedtime every night. And after a good night's sleep, notice any messages from IS embedded in your sweet dreams.

Write Yourself Right

One tried-and-true way to process your thoughts and feelings and connect with IS is putting pen to paper, or fingers to keyboard, as the case may be. It may sound like a middle-school homework assignment and yet—it's more like a magic carpet ride to clarity. Write about your experience of the current moment, the past, the future, where you feel stuck, a new breakthrough, or whatever comes to mind.

For extra credit, write about things you're grateful for, which might include your journal. Journaling is a proven technique for off-loading stress and worries, boosting mood, cleaning up your perspective, and even helping you sleep. And remember, what you write about stays between you and your Infinite Source.

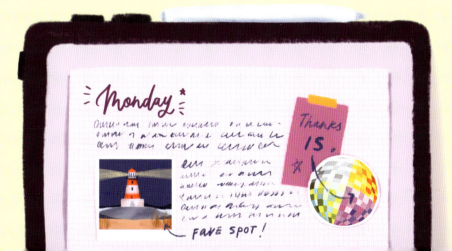

Incarnate Source:
The Divine in Form

Welcome home, party people! This is Planet Earth. Take a good look around. It's familiar territory for sure.

Chances are pretty good you've never known anything else. Unless . . . there's something you want to share?

Earth makes an epic party pad, no doubt. Yet have you considered how the ground beneath your dancing feet connects you to all that IS? It's worth repeating: You are created from stellar matter, rock star. At the same time, you are an animal. Time to celebrate your connection to this epic outdoor amphitheater.

Pretty much anyone, from the atheist to the ultradevout, can relate to feeling spiritual in nature. Maybe that's because every breath you take contains atoms that have existed from the time Earth was born, even beyond that. We have a cosmic connection. Nature is what you're made of, how it all works, and where you hang out. Plus, the intricate web of life you're an important part of is maybe the most dynamic, creative, and beautiful work of art in the world. Wait, it IS the world.

What draws you to nature, besides your people? *Homo sapiens* are cool, but we've only been around like 0.0067% of the time Earth has been spinning. That's like the last beat drop in the final song of a twelve-hour playlist. It makes sense we'd seek community with all forms of life while looking to learn from the wisdom keepers in nature. Incarnate Source is your living library. What can this ancient intelligence teach you? And how do you relate intimately with your vast planetary playground?

Despite the fact that humans are relatively new to Earth, you gotta know that you and your crew make a difference. Every dance step has a ripple effect that impacts the whole environment. If you're a science whiz, you know about the butterfly effect. It illustrates how a tiny action like a butterfly flapping its wings can set off a chain of events that eventually lead to a major outcome, like a storm forming far away. Wild, right? The interdependence of your ecosystem is affected by all other elements, just like an album is the sum of every sound. This means you, too.

Sweet Escape

You don't have to be a total hippie to get that it benefits you to be in nature. When you go outdoors and get moving, do you feel more alive? Do your spirits rise in awe? Does your Infinite Self fist-bump your Incarnate Self for taking it on a field trip? You bet.

Getting up close and personal with nature feels invigorating, divine, and inspiring because you're synching up with the energy that created you. How you like to do so depends on your flavor of DIY. A mindful hike through the forest soaking in the scent of cedar, rustle of leaves, and patches of sunlight can lower cortisol, reduce blood pressure, and reset your nervous system. Likewise, a chill walk on the beach at sunset listening to the rhythm of the waves can calm your mind and release serotonin. Nature is healing. It can be therapeutic if you're open to it.

If you're more of a thrill seeker, think of the rush you get catching some fresh alpine air as you're skiing or mountain biking. That's the flood of endorphins and dopamine kicking in. Nature doesn't just lift us up metaphorically—it stirs our biochemistry, inviting us to move, breathe, and connect to something bigger, giving us health, joy, and a renewed sense of wonder.

Homeschooling

Nature, our greatest teacher, has mastered the art of balance and beauty, function and form. You probably know bees are essential, but did you ever consider the perfection of the honeycomb? With its efficient hexagonal grid, it models a design so strong yet so light that it's been copied for use in everything from airplanes to helmets, adding strength without extra weight.

Consider the *Fibonacci sequence* as a master class in form. This mathematical pattern appears throughout nature—in the arrangements of leaves, the spirals of sunflowers, and the shells of nautiluses—offering a blueprint of adaptability and balance. Humanity has drawn inspiration from these natural geometries, applying them to art and architecture, such as the Guggenheim Museum designed by Frank Lloyd Wright. These designs echo a deeper wisdom, connecting us to nature's rhythms and reminding us that many of our own innovations have roots in the elegant structures found all around us.

Nature is the ultimate DJ of color, pattern, and shape and a mystical impetus for creators of all kinds. The Mandarinfish, with its vivid, swirling blues, greens, and oranges, may play muse to a designer who creates a fashion-foward fabric. An engineer might be equally inspired by crystals and minerals, formed over millennia, displaying geometric shapes and gradients that defy imitation. Nature is truly the OG artist and architect, weaving together beauty and purpose, color and form, teaching us that the most captivating designs often come from simply observing and honoring the world around us.

Just as honeycombs demonstrate the strength in balance and efficient use of resources, the changing seasons teach us to honor the rhythmic pattern of growth, rest, and renewal. Spring's rebirth, summer's vitality, autumn's release, and winter's quiet remind us that each phase has its purpose, echoing the cycles of life, death, and rebirth that play out.

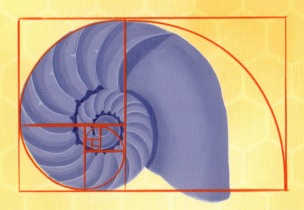

Weather Report

Unpredictable elements teach us profound lessons. The sheer might of a tornado spiraling through open plains or the deep rumble of thunder reverberating in your chest is enough to remind you of the limits of human influence and the awesome scale of the natural world. Tsunami waves crashing against cliffs exhibit raw energy, urging earthlings to respect nature's boundless strength. A snowfall blankets the world in silence and serenity, inviting introspection and wonder. Lightning's sudden burst of light in a darkened sky feels like evidence of the divine, a fleeting glimpse of nature's electrifying spirit. These are all reminders of a force far beyond human control that humbles, inspires, and reconnects.

Earth, Wind, and Fire

The elements of nature each carry energy, wisdom, and a means of divine connection. While earth is an icon of stability and resilience, wind is an ever-changing force. While oxygen-rich air is essential for life, wind reveals the extreme range of impact its form can take.

Think of the welcome brush of a breeze versus the raw power of a hurricane. If you're a sailor, ultimate Frisbee player, or hang glider, wind is a game changer. It is freedom in form. Wind also demonstrates the balance between opposing forces. Consider how wind at your back carries you forward versus wind blowing against you, which creates resistance and challenges you to step up. These contrasting influences are a great reminder of the Taoist concept of yin-yang, the idea that opposing aspects of life balance each other to create harmony.

Fire gives warmth, light, and life. It's a primal force that draws people together, sparks creativity, and reminds us of transformation and renewal. By respecting and connecting with nature's elements, we awaken to a sense of unity, experiencing a spirituality rooted in the awe, wisdom, and interdependence of life itself.

Add Water

Geeking out on water is a great way to jump into the deep end and learn from Incarnate Source's fourth element. Did you know the average person is made up of at least 60% water? Not that you're average; you're made of stardust, but still, you're mostly H_2O. And let's not forget the pacifying sloshes of embryonic fluid that ushered you in, baby.

So what does water have to teach you? Just to dip your toe in, here are a few biggies: Water, with its capacity to cleanse and renew, can lower stress, boost endorphins, and ease the mind when you immerse, grounding you in the present and washing away your worries.

The purifying aspects of water may be apparent, but not so well-known are the secrets held in the depths of the sea. Its vast reach beyond the horizon is a gorgeous reminder of infinite possibilities. How pretty saltwater looks from the shore, sparkling under the sunlight, with foamy fringed waves rolling in. Take a swim in the sea, float in a lake, wade in a stream, or take a soak in the tub, and reap the benefits of hydrotherapy while you immerse in the embrace of Incarnate Source.

What we've discovered so far in the depths of the ocean is astounding and yet remains more than 95% unexplored. This isn't so unlike yourself. You have a persona you transmit. But what lies beneath your skin, well, that's a little-known universe.

Easy Does It

Flowing water elegantly models the power of subtle persistence. The landscapes you admire are largely formed by your pal, H_2O. You might look at a uniquely shaped boulder and wonder, *What kind of superpower sculptor could possibly be strong enough to carve that out?* You guessed it—the gentle but consistent caress of water against rocks over time created that masterpiece. Fun fact: The Grand Canyon exists thanks to the Colorado River having carved it out over five million years, give or take a million.

In other words, you don't have to hit hard with a hammer to have an impact. What you do softly and consistently over time may be more powerful than an act of brute force. Slowly but surely gets you where you want to be. Even in our fast-paced world, some things can't be rushed. Or shouldn't be. This goes for problem-solving. When you feel stuck, confused, or frustrated, emulate Mother Nature and give yourself some time. Spiritual guru Lao Tzu said, "Do you have the patience to wait until your mud settles and the water is clear?"

Invite:
Take Me to Church

Chances are, you're not getting thine arse to the nearest temple, mosque, or cathedral on the regular. If you are, much respect. Regardless, worshiping outdoors can be next level because you're getting a big hug from your originating energy. You can do this anywhere in nature, but it's reassuring to have a sacred place to post up.

1. Shop around for your sanctuary. Assuming you don't live around the corner from Igauzu Falls in Argentina or Cathedral Rock in Sedona, you might need to hunt for a favorite outdoor sanctuary. Visit a few nearby spots outdoors that call to you.

2. Pick your spot. Explore different places to sit or lie down—a tree stump, a granite boulder, a grassy patch—until you find one that clicks. Look for a comfortable, private, and memorable spot—somewhere that's easy to find again and again. Settle in.

3. Immerse in the moment. As you ease into your seat, dial into the present. This is a time for quiet contemplation—maybe even meditation. That's your call. Become attuned to all the life happening in all its forms everywhere around you.

4. Cycle through your senses one by one. Let your eyes search out some point of intrigue near and far. Next, close your eyes and listen to the symphony of sounds that surrounds you. There's a lot going on out there, eh? Take a deep breath. Can you pick up any scents in nature? Take a peek now at the myriad textures nearby and sample a few. Fantastical and entertaining as they may be, immersive art installations like Meow Wolf can't hold a candle to the mind-bending eye candy on display far and wide outside the building. Ever taken a close look at a Jerusalem cricket?

5. Harmonize your frequency to Incarnate Source. Now go deeper. See if you can locate your inner spark. You may identify a physical placement, perhaps in your heart or at the crown of your head. You might feel slight tingles, like champagne bubbles releasing. Whatever the signal, see if you can experience a merging with your natural surroundings, sinking into the scenery seamlessly.

6. Communicate. Having made contact with your Infinite Self, might as well invite Infinite Source to the party. Incarnate Source is the most generous host, so make it a habit to RSVP yes on repeat.

MYSTIC MIXTAPE FOR INCARNATE SOURCE

11:11

1/365

Relax
Piano music
Rest and Relaxation

24:00

7:00

Menu

winning ways to
connect with **IS** daily

Savor Every Breath You Take

Next time you're outside enjoying some fresh air, take several deep breaths. Notice what happens when you breathe intentionally for at least one full minute. How do you feel? Refreshed? Alive? Renewed? You're tapping into one of nature's most powerful gifts—the cleansing power of oxygen. Breathing deeply calms the mind and resets the body. Studies show that deep, purposeful breathing can reduce cortisol levels, lower blood pressure, and even help you think more clearly. And if you breathe near an ocean, river, mountain, or waterfall, the air's more prevalent negative ions can boost your mood, create clarity, and promote vitality.

Build a Bridge with Love

Take care of your planet like it's the divine in form. Because if your DIY spirituality includes the idea of oneness with all that IS, then this is true. Every bit of effort you make, from a smog check to a shorter shower, helps. But what really matters is a reframe on your relationship with your Mother. Follow in the footsteps of our indigenous ancestors, and instead of objectifying nature, consider her part of your family. Acknowledge the redwoods as your cousins instead of your next coffee table. Let this intentional mindset shift guide your daily decisions, from eating local to thrifting your threads.

Lose Yourself

Naturally, you're gonna feel lost sometimes. But check this out—you can find yourself through losing yourself in nature. Step into the outdoors, leave your to-do list behind, and shed the weight of your ego. Roam around the world when you get the chance.

Wander the walkways of the insanely colorful Grand Prismatic Spring in Yellowstone National Park and check out the majestic bison nearby. Go bold with a trip to the beaches of Bali, where you can snorkel with laid-back sea turtles. Or venture Down Under to see Ulura, a.k.a. Ayers Rock, where you might spot a red kangaroo. With your focus on all the wondrous forms of nature around you near and far, your problems are put into perspective and life streams discovery.

Sing in the Rain

Living under a roof and between four walls means you probably miss some spectacular events, like lunar rainbows, morning glories opening at dawn, dew patterns on blades of grass, passing cloud formations, shooting meteors, the nocturnal call of a whippoorwill, a coyote chorus, and on and on. By becoming aware of what's happening outside your door 24/7, you can excite in phenomena more actual than the internet. Find one natural marvel a day to humbly celebrate and be in awe of, be it the sound of crickets, the sight of the sunrise, the taste of an heirloom tomato, the touch of tree bark, or the smell of blooming jasmine. Take in the universe doing its thing.

Learn from Nature's TAs

Beyond Fido, notice what animated messengers cross your path or catch your notice. Your spiritual connection to other living creatures is real, so pay attention and search for meaning. Animals can teach us volumes about presence, trust, and the simple joy of being. In various cultural traditions, for example, the spider, often seen as a symbol of creative potential and patience, serves as a reminder to carefully weave and shape your own path. The owl, known for its ability to see in the dark, embodies intuition, inner wisdom, and insight, encouraging you to look beyond the surface. Meanwhile, the octopus teaches adaptability, resilience, intelligence, and the power of transformation, demonstrating strength, flexibility, and self-reinvention.

Challenge yourself to spend a few minutes every day observing or interacting with a new critter. Show kindness and appreciation. Nature's teaching assistants don't get paid.

Give Music Therapy

A quick and easy, mutually beneficial way to connect to Incarnate Source is to talk to a houseplant. Crazy as it sounds, it's actually not. Your green friend might not have ears, but it responds to sound. The vibration and frequency of sound waves stimulate growth, promoting stronger roots and enhanced nutrient absorption. Whether it's the gentle tones of birdsong, the warmth of your voice, or soothing music, these sounds help your plant to thrive.

Bonus: When you talk to your plant, sing in your garden, or shout in the forest, you're giving flora the carbon dioxide they crave. In return, through photosynthesis, they release fresh oxygen back at you. Reciprocity at its finest. The next time you're sipping a glass of wine, consider whether those vines might have grown up vibing to Mozart or Bach. Rock me, Amadeus.

Try the
Spin Cycle

Like a playlist set on repeat, nature moves in cycles, all looping back around: the waxing and waning of the moon, the rings of a tree, the migratory patterns of monarchs, the recurring seasons in predictable order. These elements hint at a greater rhythm—a balance between creation and destruction, light and dark, stillness and movement, illness and healing. Nature's intelligent design offers a connection to rhythms older and more profound than yourself. By observing and respecting these cycles, you can accept the inevitable struggles with the victories. At the start of every day, remind yourself to live with resilience and reverence for a connection to a larger whole that sustains and inspires.

Rock Your Path

Now that you've visited the four corners of the Divine Disco Ball, you should be dancing. From breaking it down, to building it up, to stomping it out, you can go your own way. You get to decide how to chart your own DIY spiritual path. For your send-off, consider which Divine Disco Ball quadrant needs attention for now; typically, it's the corner that isn't on your radar. At some point, you'll visit them all. It's also fun and enlightening to view them in various combos. Sometimes a blend can be just the fix you need.

You can think of the Divine Disco Ball as a compass, helping you get from where you are now to where you want, or need, to be. In the combos that follow, **detours** can be thought of as what might happen if you fall out of touch with IS, stumble off your personal path, or become lost. It's going to happen, unless you're 100% enlightened. Just get back on track. The **destination** is where you want to arrive. And the **direction** is how to get there. If you come up with a better riff, go with that. The jam sesh to follow is your call. These Spark Starters are just samples to prompt your further inquiry into the great mystery. Check out these dynamic duos and a final ensemble number to take you out on a high note.

Spark Starter Kit

Infinite Self + Incarnate Self

Detour: identity crisis, social anxiety, imposter syndrome, confusion, indecision, feeling fragmented

Destination: authenticity, alignment, integration, intuition, self-actualization, self-compassion

Direction: It can be profoundly unsettling to feel uneasy in your own skin. Whether due to negative beliefs, insecurities, social expectations, new situations, unexpected curveballs, or heck, even hormones, this is when you need a straight shot to the Self half of the Divine Disco Ball.

What happens when you connect your nonphysical, spiritual nature with your physical mind-body package? You are a whole person, actually. You're in touch with your deepest truth and you act accordingly. Authenticity is your jam. Your mind-body functions in accordance with your higher self. If you're in touch with yourself from the inside out and know and accept your strengths and weaknesses, you will feel the congruence of integration. Your thoughts, feelings, and actions will align with the whole person you know yourself to be. Unafraid to look at the

dark and the light within you, you can identify the places that need work and attend to them with understanding, self-love, and responsibility. This wilderness of personal growth includes your physical, emotional, mental, and spiritual facets, and it's wide open for continuous discovery. When you get that, progressing toward the most integrated version of yourself is everything, you're ready to glow up.

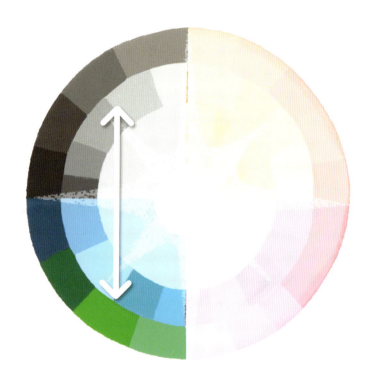

Infinite Source + Incarnate Source

Detour: stress, boredom, uncertainty, overwhelm, victim consciousness, narcissism

Destination: awe, beauty, healthy humility, support, devotion, gratitude

Direction: There's a reason why so many Indigenous traditions seek healing and truth by taking long periods of time alone in nature. The Australian Aboriginals call it a Walkabout, and the Sami of northern Scandinavia call it "going to the wilderness." You don't have to make a run for the hills, but if you're feeling over it, Source is your antidote. Quiet solitude reconnects your spirit with Infinite Source, while time with Incarnate Source makes your soul feel right at home.

To tease you into paying attention to stuff beyond the self, nature surrounds you to astound you. If you're a fan of beauty, the great outdoors has even more to be grateful for than all that's available on Amazon. It's right outside for you to enjoy—and it's never the same twice, just to keep you consuming. For doubters and skeptics that Infinite Source is even a thing, your epic dance floor awaits to point to the unfathomable.

The Source side of the Divine Disco Ball puts life into perspective. Lighten up, be curious and thankful, receive divine support, stay spiritually connected, and live in wonder.

Incarnate Source + Incarnate Self

Detour: ungrounded, in your own head too much, spaced out, disembodied, stagnate

Destination: adventure, grounding, vitality, sensuality, physicality, mindful movement

Direction: The playground of Planet Earth is where you get anchored, where all your senses merge to help you feel rooted and connected to your Incarnate Self and Source. This is where you come for stability, healthy vibes, pleasure, and play. So if you're feeling heady or detached, it's time to get physical in nature to help balance you out.

The love affair between you and your boogie wonderland is a match made in heaven. Doesn't it just make you want to do a cartwheel in the grass? What are your favorite ways to get active in nature? A walk in the rain? Snowboarding down a mountain piled with sparkly white powder? A boardwalk bike ride? Nature beckons us to commune, and she is irresistible. When your heart gets pumping as you explore the delights on offer out there, you're in the zone. Activities like fly-fishing, hiking, or planting basil in your herb garden, done mindfully, are forms of worship. You can dance if you want to in your own front yard. Celebrating and enjoying nature with your body-mind is lively, immersive, and ecstatic.

Infinite Source + Infinite Self

Detour: hopelessness, burnout, loneliness, scarcity, apathy, the weight of the world on your shoulders

Destination: cosmic consciousness, truth, trust, meaning, relief, bliss

Direction: When your compass is off-kilter and you feel directionless, look up. Moving closer to the Infinite means finding optimism where you thought you'd lost it, meaning where you thought there was nothing much to care about, abundance where you'd felt lack, and peace where there was pain. A trip to the lofty quadrants can be the quantum shift you need, whether you engage for five minutes a day or a five-day silent retreat. It's healing, hopeful, and harmonizing. This is a communion of illumination. As out-there as it might seem, finding spiritual alignment ironically makes you feel more solid. When your will and divine will are one, you have a sense of purpose.

For a shortcut to the nonphysical realm, you might want to sample some classic spiritual traditions and sacred texts. Exploring what's out there can add richness and depth to your repertoire. Stay curious and investigate with an open mind. Add to that your own firsthand experience, and acknowledge and appreciate psychic insights, serendipitous experiences, or intuitive wisdom you can't explain. However it presents itself, you are steeped in the spiritual realm, and it feels fine.

Infinite Source + Incarnate Self

Detour: disconnection, insecurity, self-criticism, feeling blocked, frustration, impatience

Destination: grace, miracles, surrender, clarity, security, faith

Direction: Adulting can be mildly soul-crushing at times. When you have a never-ending task list that just keeps growing, it can be hard to find your Infinite Self. However, you can always call on Infinite Source. That's any old time: when you're not feeling so spiritual, when you're stuck, or when you know what you want but you don't have a clue how to get it.

This is where faith comes in. When logic wants to work out a problem over which you have no control, how do you explain the option to hand it over to IS? We have feebly created language to describe the divine acting in our lives. It's grace, showing itself in what we call miracles. You can cocreate with IS in a dance of intention, action, and surrender. The more you involve IS in your challenging and celebratory times, the better it gets. Can the know-it-all ego leave some space for divine intervention? Could that door slamming in your face be IS doing you a cosmic favor? Oh, that's nothing. You don't even know what goes on behind the scenes on your behalf. Even what blocks the path is the path.

Infinite Self + Incarnate Source

Detour: self-absorbed, screen fatigue, eco-anxiety, cabin fever, restlessness, negativity

Destination: oneness, inspiration, acceptance, resonance, freedom, perspective

Direction: One side effect of being self-absorbed or constricted is that you may not be aware of it. If you wake up with this realization, take a diagonal route across the Divine Disco Ball. The remedy is to get out of your head and into nature. Seek sunlight, instead of blue light. Tune into the relief of natural rhythms. Ask your inner wisdom for answers, instead of a search engine.

When your Infinite Self joins with Incarnate Source, you are absorbed in the natural order of things. Lighten up and join the expansive flow of the natural world. It's easy to get fixated on physical form. After all, you were born to be alive. Why not make the most of it? But that includes tending to your timeless soul and limitless spirit. A mindful meander outside or meditation in fresh air will set you straight. Dark thoughts lift in the light of the sun and moon. You are inseparable from the whole cosmic symphony. And your soulful notes strike just the right chord.

Infinite Source & Self + Incarnate Source & Self

Detour: imbalance, alienation, chaos, fear, addiction, despair

Destination: love, peace, wholeness, equanimity, presence, enlightenment

Direction: When everything comes together, it feels chill. Held by IS, anchored in you—your own bestie—dazzled by your surroundings, and lit from within, you are vibing with the universe. You don't have to grasp for wholeness because you feel it deep down, even as upheaval swirls out there. Peace pervades, no matter what's up now. You're dazzled by all that you're a part of and it reflects back—you are dazzling in your dazzling-ness. With the knowledge that it's all unfolding as it should, at least in some unseen meta way, you're free to enjoy and relax. What's to do, besides all the obvious things, but love?

Love your Source and yourself, even as the universe loves you regardless. The abundant love that fills you up spills over onto all the particles, people, and places you come across. Lead with love, live in love, and leave a trail of love. It's the oxygen between you and your world that keeps the sparks lit and the formula that turns flames into fireworks.

3, 2, 1, 1, 1, 1 . . . Blast Off

Time to launch, shining star. You're equipped with a compass, a solid playlist, and classic hits of inspiration, so you're set to go your own way. And in your empowered state, have you noticed that DIY is kind of a misnomer? Because, when it comes to spirituality, you actually don't have to do it yourself. You're always dancing with fellow creatures, breathing alongside plants, vibing with energy, and in sync with the universe. You're never alone. The divine you seek has been with you all the time.

Rock your path.

Thank You

Fresh-Eric, for valuing hard work, celebrating nature, and nudging me when it's low tide.

My indispensable editor Marisa Solis, for her patience, commitment, and freakishly cunning writer whispering. And her stellar sidekick Elizabeth Dougherty, who seamlessly stepped in to finish what we started, heroically and in sync.

Doriana Del Pilar, for being as conceptually on point as she is artistically skilled, and for getting it, 100%. Our partnership = IS in Charge. And Rachel Lopez Metzger, for masterfully mixing harmony between words and visuals.

The inspiring team at The Collective Book Studio, including Angela Engel, Elizabeth Saake, and Amy Treadwell for their enthusiasm, wisdom, talent, and expertise. Rock on.

My mom and dad, for all the things.

My sons, Max and Ned, for being authentic in their spirituality and everything else.

Sharp-eyed early readers, including Olivia, Zach, Emma, Ned, Kaitlynn, Max, and Rya.

And IS, behind it all.

Contributors

Artist Doriana Del Pilar is an illustrator, architect, and faculty teacher from Santo Domingo, Dominican Republic. Passionate about art and color, and inspired by her Dominican culture and deep faith, she finds joy in creating from a place of reflection, gratitude and connection. Her illustrations are influenced by everyday moments, cultural traditions, and personal experience. Doriana illustrated the books *Mi Camino Positivo*, a memoir of life stories and reflections by Cesarina Benavides, and *Gael's First Meal*.

Editor Marisa Solis is a book coach and developmental editor with more than 25 years in publishing. Her passion is helping people conceptualize, refine, and write their best book. Staple ingredients in Marisa's spiritual practice include heeding synchronicities and hiking in nature. Her forthcoming book is *From Expert to Author: Transform Your Nonfiction Book Idea into a Finished Manuscript*.

About the Author

Author and spiritual guide Faith Freed is a licensed psychotherapist who brings more than 15 years of clinical experience and two advanced degrees to her private practice, writing, and business. She specializes in personal and spiritual growth, helping people find clarity, confidence, and connection. Faith's previous books include *IS: Your Authentic Spirituality Unleashed* and *Starting Therapy: A Guide to Getting Ready, Feeling Informed, and Gaining the Most from Your Sessions*. Faith is the founder of Freed-Om, a company dedicated to inspiration, DIY spirituality, and authentic self-expression. You can learn more at DIYSpirituality.com.